Photography by:
Michael Neugebauer

CHIMPANZEE FAMILY
Jane Goodall

A MADISON MINI BOOK

Published by Madison Marketing Limited.
Madison Marketing Limited holds the exclusive
license to this edition.
Copyright © 1991 by Neugebauer Rights & Licenses AG., Zurich.
Text copyright © 1991 by Jane Goodall.
All rights reserved.
ISBN 1-55066-013-6

Printed in Canada

Printed on recycled paper

CHIMPANZEE FAMILY

Jane Goodall

ANIMAL SERIES

Photographs selected by
Michael Neugebauer

Madison Marketing Limited

This is Fifi with her daughters, 4 year old Flossi and 9 year old Fanni. Chimpanzee mothers love their infants very much, and continue to care for them as the children grow up.

Fifi's two older sons, Frodo and Freud, still like to spend a lot of time with their mother. Fifi and her family live in Gombe National Park, Tanzania, where I have been watching chimpanzees since 1960. Fifi was just an infant then. Now she is about 30 years old.

There are about 45 chimpanzees in Fifi's group, and they all know each other. Sometimes they get together to feed on delicious fruits. It's like a big party. The adults call loudly and charge about in excitement while the young ones play, chasing each other through the trees and on the ground. Then they all settle down to feed.

When they feel full and contented, they sit comfortably and groom each other. They pick out little bits of dry skin or small ticks. This grooming doesn't just keep their coats clean – the gentle, stroking movements make them relax. After a while they take a nap.

Chimpanzee mothers spend a lot of time away from the group, just with their own families. Fifi is a very playful female and is always ready for a game with her daughters. They tickle each other, just like we do, and laugh.

Soon another young mother joins Fifi for a while. This is Gremlin, with her little son Galahad, who is five months old. Galahad is just learning to walk and climb. Gremlin makes sure that he stays close by so she can rescue him quickly if he gets into trouble.

Gremlin has an older brother named Goblin. I first met him when he was a tiny baby. Now he is the boss male. There are five other big males in the group, and they all respect Goblin. The males protect the land where Fifi, Gremlin and all the others live, so that they can feel safe.

Fifi does not stay with Gremlin and Goblin for long. She sets off again, and she and her daughters climb to feed on figs. Chimpanzees like all different kinds of foods. Leaves and flowers and stems and bark. Also insects and, sometimes, meat. But they eat more fruit than anything else.

Chimps are like us in a lot of ways. When they greet they hug and kiss. When one is frightened or sad his friend comforts him by patting his back or holding his hand. They can think and work out problems, like how to feed on the termites under the ground. They use blades of grass or little twigs as tools. The termites bite on, the chimp pulls out the tool – and then picks the termites off. The young ones learn by watching their mothers.

Flossi is tired after her long, busy day and Fifi carries her on her back. She rides there like a little jockey. Soon Fifi will make a nest for the night – a comfortable platform of leafy branches. Flossi will snuggle up with her mother. Fanni will make her own little nest nearby.

The chimpanzees at Gombe are lucky, for they are protected. In other parts of Africa the forests are being cut down. People want to build houses there or grow crops. And they sell the trees for timber. Some people hunt chimps to eat them. And sometimes they shoot the mothers to capture the babies for zoos, or circuses, or for research. That is very cruel.

The chimpanzees need all the help we can give them or before too long they will all be gone from the wild.

*J*ANE GOODALL has shared her important discoveries and her love of animals with millions of people around the world through books, films and lectures. She has founded ongoing research and educational institutes on two continents, and is one of the world's most acclaimed naturalists.

The Jane Goodall Institute for Wildlife
Research, Education and Conservation
P.O. Box 41720, Tucson, AZ 85717 U.S.A.

The Jane Goodall Institute — Canada
P.O. Box 3125, Station "C"
Ottawa, Ontario K1Y 4J4 Canada

The Jane Goodall Institute — U.K.
15 Clarendon Park
Lymington, Hants SO41 8AX United Kingdom